5A

CHATTO POETS FOR THE YOUNG

The Apple-Raid
and Other Poems

CHATTO POETS FOR THE YOUNG
General Editor: LEONARD CLARK

MICHAEL BALDWIN *Hob and Other Poems*
LEONARD CLARK *Secret as Toads*
D. J. ENRIGHT *Rhyme Times Rhyme*
JOHN FULLER *Squeaking Crust*
PHOEBE HESKETH *A Song of Sunlight*
EDWARD LOWBURY *Green Magic*
VERNON SCANNELL *The Apple-Raid and Other Poems*
R. S. THOMAS *Young and Old*

The Apple-Raid and other Poems

BY

VERNON SCANNELL

CHATTO & WINDUS
LONDON

Published by
Chatto & Windus Ltd
40 William IV Street
London WC2N 4DF

*

Clarke, Irwin & Co. Ltd.
Toronto

All rights reserved. No part of this publication
may be reproduced, stored in a retrieval system,
or transmitted, in any form, or by any means,
electronic, mechanical, photocopying, recording
or otherwise, without the prior permission of
Chatto & Windus Ltd.

ISBN 0 7011 5044 0

© Vernon Scannell 1974

Printed in Great Britain by
REDWOOD BURN LIMITED
Trowbridge & Esher

Contents

First Fight	page 7
The Climb and the Dream	12
Intelligence Test	14
Sunday in June	15
November Story	16
Poem on Bread	18
Makers and Creatures	19
Death of a Snowman	20
Epitaph for a Bad Soldier	21
Elegy for a Countryman	22
The Apple-Raid	23
I Bit an Apple	24
The Music of Sunday	25
Washing Day	26
Cat	27
The Lady and the Gypsy	28
Snow Dream	29
The Captive's Song	30
View from a High Chair	31
Last Fight	32

FIRST FIGHT

I
Tonight, then, is the night;
Stretched on the massage table,
Wrapped in his robe, he breathes
Liniment and sweat
And tries to close his ears
To the roaring of the crowd,
A murky sea of noise
That bears upon its tide
The frail sound of the bell
And brings the cunning fear
That he might not do well,
Not fear of bodily pain
But that his tight-lipped pride
Might be sent crashing down,
His white ambition slain,
Knocked spinning the glittering crown.
How could his spirit bear
That ignominious fall?
Not hero but a clown
Spurned or scorned by all.
The thought appals, and he
Feels sudden envy for
The roaring crowd outside
And wishes he were there,
Anonymous and safe,
Calm in the tolerant air,
Would almost choose to be
Anywhere but here.

II
The door blares open suddenly,
The room is sluiced with row;
His second says, 'We're on next fight,

We'd better get going now.
You got your gumshield, haven't you?
Just loosen up — that's right —
Don't worry Boy, you'll be okay
Once you start to fight.'

Out of the dressing room, along
The neutral passage to
The yelling cavern where the ring
Through the haze of blue
Tobacco smoke is whitewashed by
The aching glare of light:
Geometric ropes are stretched as taut
As this boy's nerves are tight.

And now he's in his corner where
He tries to look at ease;
He feels the crowd's sharp eyes as they
Prick and pry and tease;
He hears them murmur like the sea
Or some great dynamo:
They are not hostile yet they wish
To see his lifeblood flow.
His adversary enters now;
The Boy risks one quick glance;
He does not see an enemy
But something there by chance,
Not human even, but a cold
Abstraction to defeat,
A problem to be solved by guile,
Quick hands and knowing feet.
The fighters' names are shouted out;
They leave their corners for
The touch of gloves and brief commands;
The disciplines of war.
Back in their corners, stripped of robes,

They hear the bell clang one
Brazen syllable which says
The battle has begun.

III
Bite on gumshield,
Guard held high,
The crowd are silenced,
All sounds die.
Lead with the left,
Again, again;
Watch for the opening,
Feint and then
Hook to the body
But he's blocked it and
Slammed you back
With a fierce right hand.
Hang on grimly,
The fog will clear,
Sweat in your nostrils,
Grease and fear.
You're hurt and staggering,
Shocked to know
That the story's altered:
He's the hero!

But the mist is clearing,
The referee snaps
A rapid warning
And he smartly taps
Your hugging elbow
And then you step back
Ready to counter
The next attack,
But the first round finishes
Without mishap.

You suck in the air
From the towel's skilled flap.
A voice speaks urgently
Close to your ear:
'Keep your left going, Boy,
Stop him getting near.
He wants to get close to you,
So jab him off hard;
When he tries to slip below,
Never mind your guard,
Crack him with a solid right,
Hit him on the chin,
A couple downstairs
And then he'll pack it in.'

Slip in the gumshield
Bite on it hard,
Keep him off with your left,
Never drop your guard.
Try a left hook,
But he crosses with a right
Smack on your jaw
And Guy Fawkes' Night
Flashes and dazzles
Inside your skull,
Your knees go bandy
And you almost fall.
Keep the left jabbing,
Move around the ring,
Don't let him catch you with
Another hook or swing.
Keep your left working,
Keep it up high,
Stab it out straight and hard,
Again — above the eye.
Sweat in the nostrils,

But nothing now of fear,
You're moving smooth and confident
In comfortable gear.
Jab with the left again,
Quickly move away;
Feint and stab another in,
See him duck and sway.
Now for the pay-off punch,
Smash it hard inside;
It thuds against his jaw, he falls,
Limbs spread wide.
And suddenly you hear the roar,
Hoarse music of the crowd,
Voicing your hot ecstasy,
Triumphant, male and proud.

IV
Now, in the sleepless darkness of his room
The Boy, in bed, remembers. Suddenly
The victory tastes sour. The man he fought
Was not a thing, as lifeless as a broom,
He was a man who hoped and trembled too;
What of him now? What was *he* going through?
And then The Boy bites hard on resolution:
Fighters can't pack pity with their gear,
And yet a bitter taste stays with the notion;
He's forced to swallow down one treacherous tear.
But that's the last. He is a boy no longer;
He is a man, a fighter, such as jeer
At those who make salt beads with melting eyes,
Whatever might cry out, is hurt, or dies.

THE CLIMB AND THE DREAM

The boy had never seen the tree before;
He thought it was a splendid one to climb,
The branches strong enough to take far more
Than his slight weight; and, while they did not rhyme
In perfect echoes of each other's shape,
They were arranged in useful patterns which
He found as thrilling as a fire-escape.
Now was his chance! He hopped across the ditch
And wriggled underneath the rusty wire,
And then he found himself confronted by
The lofty challenge, suddenly much higher
Now he was at its foot. He saw the sky
Through foliage and branches, broken like
A pale blue china plate. He leapt and clung
To the lowest branch and swung from left to right,
Then heaved himself astride the swaying rung.
With cautious hands and feet he made a start
From branch to branch; dust tickled in his throat.
He smelt the dark green scent of leaf and bark;
Malicious thorny fingers clutched his coat
And once clawed at his forehead, drawing blood.
Sweat drenched his aching body, blurred his eyes,
But he climbed up and up until he stood
Proud on the highest bough and, with surprise,
Looked down to see the shrunken fields and streams
As if his climb had re-created them;
And he was sure that, often, future dreams
Would bring this vision back to him. But then
A sudden darkening came upon the sky,
He felt the breeze grow burlier and chill,
Joy drained away. And then he realised why:
This was a tree he'd scaled, and not a hill —
The journey down would not be easier
But much more difficult than his ascent:

The foothold surfaces seemed greasier
And less accessible, and he had spent
Much of his strength, was very close to tears,
And sick with fear, yet knew he must go down.
The thing he dreamt about in after-years
Was not the moment when he wore the crown
Of gold achievement on the highest bough
Above the common world of strife and pain,
But the ordeal of dark descent, and how
He sobbed with joy to reach safe earth again.

INTELLIGENCE TEST

'What do you use your eyes for?'
The white-coated man enquired.
'I use my eyes for looking,'
Said Toby, '—unless I'm tired.'

'I see. And then you close them,'
Observed the white-coated man.
'Well done. A very good answer.
Let's try another one.

'What is your nose designed for?
What use is the thing to you?'
'I use my nose for smelling,'
Said Toby, 'don't you, too?'

'I do indeed,' said the expert,
'That's what the thing is for.
Now I've another question to ask you,
Then there won't be any more.

'What are your ears intended for?
Those things at each side of your head?
Come on — don't be shy — I'm sure you can say.'
'For washing behind,' Toby said.

SUNDAY IN JUNE

Windows open to salute the summer
Which enters every sleepy parlour
A green delightful scent more subtle
Than the breath of flushing petal.

Over lawns the butterflies spin
Like truant petals on the wind's whim
And flowers like sleeping butterflies hang
From slender stems, no bubbling song

Of holiday birds disturbs their dreaming
Nor tumbling bells bewildering evening;
And sweet and green in the mind's dim parlour
Flowers again the punctual summer.

NOVEMBER STORY

The evening had caught cold;
Its eyes were blurred.
It had a dripping nose
And its tongue was furred.

I sat in a warm bar
After the day's work;
November snuffled outside,
Greasing the sidewalk.

But soon I had to go
Out into the night
Where shadows prowled the alleys,
Hiding from the light.

But light shone at the corner
On the pavement where
A man had fallen over
Or been knocked down there.

His legs on the slimed concrete
Were splayed out wide;
He had been propped against a lamp-post;
His head lolled to one side.

A victim of crime or accident,
An image of fear,
He remained quite motionless
As I drew near.

Then a thin voice startled silence
From a doorway close by
Where an urchin hid from the wind:
"Spare a penny for the guy!"

I gave the boy some money
And hastened on.
A voice called, "Thank you guv'nor!"
And the words upon

The wincing air seemed strange —
So hoarse and deep —
As if the guy had spoken
In his restless sleep.

POEM ON BREAD

The poet is about to write a poem;
He does not use a pencil or a pen.
He dips his long thin finger into jam
Or something savoury preferred by men.
This poet does not choose to write on paper;
He takes a single slice of well-baked bread
And with his jam or marmite-nibbed forefinger
He writes his verses down on that instead.
His poem is fairly short as all the best are.
When he has finished it he hopes that you
Or someone else — your brother, friend or sister —
Will read and find it marvellous and true.
If you can't read, then eat: it tastes quite good.
If you do neither, all that I can say
Is he who needs no poetry or bread
Is really in a devilish bad way.

MAKERS AND CREATURES

It is a curious experience
And one you're bound to know, though probably
In other realms than that of literature,
Though I speak of poems now, assuming
That you are interested, otherwise,
Of course, you wouldn't be reading this;
It is strange to come across a poem
In a magazine or book and fail
At first to see that it's your own.
Sometimes you think, grateful and surprised,
"That's really not too bad", or gloomily:
"Many have done as well and far, far better".
Or, in despair, "My God, that's terrible.
What was I thinking of to publish it!"
And then you start to wonder how the great
Poets felt, seeing, surprised, their poems
As strangers, beautiful. And how do all the
Makers feel to see their creatures live?
The carpenter, the architect, the man who
Crochets intricate embroideries
Of steel across the sky. And how does God
Feel, looking at his poems, his creatures?
The swelling inhalation of plump hills,
Plumage of poplars on the pale horizon,
Fishleap flashing in pools cool as silver,
Great horses haunched with glossy muscles,
Birds who spray their song like apple juice,
And the soft shock of snow. He must feel good
Surprised again by these. But what happens
When he takes a look at man? Does he say,
"That's really not too bad", or does he, as I fear,
Wince once and mutter to himself:
"What was I thinking of publishing that one!"?

DEATH OF A SNOWMAN

I was awake all night,
Big as a polar bear,
Strong and firm and white.
The tall black hat I wear
Was draped with ermine fur.
I felt so fit and well
Till the world began to stir
And the morning sun swell.
I was tired, began to yawn;
At noon in the humming sun
I caught a severe warm;
My nose began to run.
My hat grew black and fell,
Was followed by my grey head.
There was no funeral bell,
But by tea-time I was dead.

EPITAPH FOR A BAD SOLDIER

No beads on the eyelash,
No crepe round the hat,
Candles and flowers,
Nor black silken sash.
Sleep sweetly my dears
And do not wake sad.
Keep your necklace of tears
For a living lad.
On his discharge-book
The seeker may find
His life summed up
By the military mind:
No angry charges
Of traitor or cad
But this plain epitaph:
Conduct — Bad.

ELEGY FOR A COUNTRYMAN

Strange that the world he loved
Should seem unmoved,
The ungloved green
Hand of the chestnut prove
Insensible to his going.

Strange that the sky he knew
Should still be doved
With softest wings of cloud,
That the branch he loved
Should sing so loud.

Strange to one conversant
With his passions
And his pointed fears
That summer struts the gayest fashions:
No Swithin's day of tears.

Not, after all, so strange,
For he has gone
To join at last his bright
Love in amorous quiet;
Right that the boughs be hung with song,
That the green bride wear this festive white.

THE APPLE-RAID

Darkness came early, though not yet cold;
Stars were strung on the telegraph wires;
Street lamps spilled pools of liquid gold;
The breeze was spiced with garden fires.

That smell of burnt leaves, the early dark,
Can still excite me but not as it did
So long ago when we met in the park —
Myself, John Peters and David Kidd.

We moved out of town to the district where
The lucky and wealthy had their homes
With garages, gardens, and apples to spare
Ripely clustered in the trees' green domes.

We chose the place we meant to plunder
And climbed the wall and dropped down to
The secret dark. Apples crunched under
Our feet as we moved through the grass and dew.

The clusters on the lower boughs of the tree
Were easy to reach. We stored the fruit
In pockets and jerseys until all three
Boys were heavy with their tasty loot.

Safe on the other side of the wall
We moved back to town and munched as we went.
I wonder if David remembers at all
That little adventure, the apples' fresh scent.

Strange to think that he's fifty years old,
That tough little boy with scabs on his knees;
Stranger to think that John Peters lies cold
In an orchard in France beneath apple trees.

I BIT AN APPLE...

I bit an apple and the flesh was sweet:
Juice tingled on the tongue and from the fruit
Arose a scent that memory received
And in a flash raised ghosts of apple trees,
Leaves blistered with minutest bulbs of rain
Bewildering an autumn drawing-room
Where carpets stained with unaccustomed shadow
Heard one old table creak, perhaps moved too
By some remembrance of a former time
When summer like a lover came to him
And laid amazing offerings at his feet.
I bit an apple and the spell was sweet.

THE MUSIC OF SUNDAY

The music of Sunday has always been sad:
The dark bells are dolorous as slowly they sway
And loll their great tongues: the Saturday singers
Have hidden their silvery ditties away.

The music of Sunday has always been sad.
My memory softens while arteries harden:
I remember dim evenings when Mother was playing,
And we watered with tears the Monastery Garden.

I remember my Father's brown baritone voice
Melodiously grieving for poor Tommy Lad;
I remember the keening of grandfather's fiddle.
The music of Sundays has always been sad.

WASHING DAY

Suds twinkle, weightless diamonds,
Glittering seeds of bled pomegranates.
Beneath the airy coruscations
The water is blue, diluted ink.
Steam sweetens the kitchen's breath,
Windows grow thoughtful, dream.
Sheets and shirts are punched and squeezed,
Wrung out and dumped
Heavy like lumps of dough
Into a dry tub,
Are heaved into the sun and hung
Uncurled on a windy sky
To ripple and swell, swank and flap:
Hygienic bunting, a celebration
Of victory, ephemeral but real.

CAT

My cat has got no name,
We simply call him Cat;
He doesn't seem to blame
Anyone for that.

For he is not like us
Who often, I'm afraid,
Kick up quite a fuss
If *our* names are mislaid.

As if, without a name,
We'd be no longer there
But like a tiny flame
Vanish in bright air.

My pet, he doesn't care
About such things as that:
Black buzz and golden stare
Require no name but Cat.

THE LADY AND THE GYPSY

I handed her my silver
And gullibility,
And tremulously asked her
Who would marry me,
For I was getting older,
Approaching twenty-three —
At least that's what I told her:
All girls, I'm sure, agree
It's sometimes right to suffer
Lapse of memory.

She told me to be patient,
But not for very long,
For down the summer pavement
As lilting as a song
Mr. Right would wander,
Eager, gallant, strong;
And sure enough last summer
My man did come along:
If he is Mr. Right, then
Give me Mr. Wrong.

SNOW DREAM

He walked upon the silent quilt of snow:
Night, a buried moon and all the stars
Swept away like cinders while the slow
Sewing of the flakes performed their dance
In spectral trillions, musicless pavan.
He was alone in the night of endless snow,
The world's most lonely, maybe its only man.
Behind, each footprint instantly filled in;
He left no trail, there was no path to follow.
If he began his own snowdance — to spin
Tranced pirouettes — when still, he would not know
Which way led forward, which would take him back.
He would not know which way he ought to go.
But neither did he now — no guide, no track,
Moonslaughter done and every star stone dead —
He drifted through the white storm in his head,
The ceaseless cancellation of the snow.

THE CAPTIVE'S SONG

The stars that are whistling above the black town
Embroider the covers where lovers lie down,
Supplying sweet sanction for all that they do,
But glitter derision for me and for you.

The far train that calls like an owl in the night
Runs straight as a fuse through the darkness to light,
Exploding in rendezvous, lucky ones who
In delight are united, unlike me and you.

The 'plane tipped with jewels of light at the wings
Sings loud in the clouds and indifferently brings
Exiles to firesides, the false to the true,
But mocks the cold distance between me and you.

Be patient my dearest, the night is in sight
When the stars and the 'plane and the train will unite
To heal separation and we shall be free
To relish the feast laid for you and for me.

VIEW FROM A HIGH CHAIR

Here thump on tray
With mug, and splash
Wet white down there.
The sofa purrs,
The window squeaks.
Bump more with mug
And make voice big
Then she will come,
Sky in the room,
Quiet as a cloud,
Flowers in the sky,
Come down snow-soft
But warm as milk,
Hide all the things
That squint with shine,
That gruff and bite
And want to hurt;
Will swallow us
And taste so sweet
As down we go
To try our feet.

LAST FIGHT

This is one you know that you can't win.
You've lost your snap, can't put the punches in
The way you used to, belting till they fell;
You'll have a job to fiddle to the bell.
One round to go; backpedal, feint and weave;
Roll with the punches, make the crowd believe
You've still got something left. Above all, go
The distance, stay there till the end, although —
Even if you clipped him on the chin —
You know that this is one that you can't win.